30p

A Little Book of Childhood

Illustrated by
Henriette Willebeek Le Mair

FREDERICK WARNE

FREDERICK WARNE

Published by the Penguin Group

Penguin Books Ltd, 27 Wrights Lane, London W8 5TZ, England

Penguin Putnam Inc., 375 Hudson Street, New York, N.Y. 10014, USA

Penguin Books Australia Ltd, Ringwood, Victoria, Australia

Penguin Books Canada Ltd, 10 Alcorn Avenue, Toronto, Ontario, Canada M4V 3B2

Penguin Books (NZ) Ltd, Private Bag 102902, NSMC, Aukland, New Zealand

Penguin Books India (P) Ltd, 11, Community Centre, Panchsheel Park, New Delhi 110 017, India

Penguin Books (South Africa) (Pty) Ltd, 5 Watkins Street, Denver Ext 4, 2094, South Africa

Penguin Books Ltd, Registered Offices: Harmondsworth, Middlesex, England

First published by Frederick Warne 2000

1 2 3 4 5 6 7 8 9 10

Original illustrations copyright © Soefi Stichting Inayat Fundatie Sirdar, 1911, 1913, 1914, 1915, 1917, 1925, 1926

New reproductions copyright © Soefi Stichting Inayat Fundatie Sirdar, 2000

Every attempt has been made to trace the copyright holders of the quotations in this book. The publishers apologise if any inadvertent omissions have been made.

ISBN 0 7232 4665 3

Colour reproduction by Anglia Graphics, Bedford, England.

Printed and bound in Singapore by Tien Wah Press (Pte) Ltd.

INTRODUCTION

Childhood is a period of our lives which we frequently look back upon with fond and joyful memories. It is a time of wild imaginings and innocence as we explore and discover the world around us and confront new experiences every day. The following pages are filled with nostalgic quotations about childhood, as well as proverbs and rhymes which remind us of the magic and wonder that childhood brings.

The first and simplest emotion which we discover
in the human mind, is curiosity.

Edmund Burke

While the cat's away,

the mice will play.

Proverb

Away down the river;

A hundred miles or more,

Other little children

Shall bring my boats ashore.

from *A Child's Garden of Verses*,
Robert Louis Stevenson

If youth knew what age would crave, it would both

get and save.

15

We say that a girl with her doll anticipates her mother. It is more true perhaps, that most mothers are still children with playthings.

Francis H. Bradley

Children are poor men's riches.

Proverb

Then she wiped her eyes with her hands, for princesses don't always have their handkerchiefs in their pockets any more than some other little girls I know of.

from *The Princess and the Goblin,*
George MacDonald

There's only one pretty child in the world, and
every mother has it.

Proverb

23

Sometimes the children ran away and pretended they didn't belong to the nurses and sometimes the nurses lagged behind and pretended they didn't belong to the children.

from *A Gallery of Children*,
A.A. Milne

24

Children are a bridge to heaven.

Proverb

... there is no friend like a sister

In calm or stormy weather.

from *Goblin Market*,
Christina Rossetti

28

Children and fools have merry lives.

Proverb

31

What are little boys made of ?

    Frogs and snails and puppy-dogs' tails,

That's what little boys are made of.

What are little girls made of?

    Sugar and spice and all that's nice,

That's what little girls are made of.

Traditional

Give me a child for the first seven years and you may do what you like with him after.

Proverb

35

A child should always say what's true

And speak when he is spoken to,

And behave mannerly at table;

At least as far as he is able.

from *A Child's Garden of Verses*,
Robert Louis Stevenson

Children should be seen and not heard.

Proverb

"Do you know who made you?"

"Nobody as I knows on," said the child, with a short laugh ... "I 'spect I growd. Don't think nobody never made me."

from *Uncle Tom's Cabin*,
Harriet Beecher Stowe

Children pick up words as pigeons peas, and utter them again as God shall please.

Proverb

Curiouser and curiouser!

from *Alice in Wonderland,*
Lewis Carroll

Joys shared with others are all the more enjoyed.

Proverb

Monday's child is fair of face,

   Tuesday's child is full of grace,

Wednesday's child is full of woe,

   Thursday's child has far to go,

Friday's child is loving and giving,

   Saturday's child must work hard for a living,

But the child that is born on Sabbath day

   Is fair and wise and good and gay.

Traditional

48

One, two, three a-leerie

Four, five, six a-leerie

Seven, eight, nine a-leerie

Ten a-leerie, skip with me.

Traditional skipping rhyme

How do you like to go up in a swing,

Up in the air so blue?

Oh, I do think it's the pleasantest thing

Ever a child can do!

from *A Child's Garden of Verses*,
Robert Louis Stevenson

Fine feathers make fine birds.

Proverb

I was a child and she was a child
In this kingdom by the sea;
But we loved with a love
That was more than love –
I and my Annabel Lee.

from *Annabel Lee*,
Edgar Allan Poe

There was a little girl who had a little curl,

Right in the middle of her forehead.

When she was good she was very very good,

But when she was bad she was horrid.

Traditional

The best smell is bread, the best savour salt, the best love that of children.

Proverb